DISNEY
PIRATES of the CARIBBEAN
AT WORLD'S END

HOW TO APPLY YOUR PIRATE TATTOOS:
1) Cut around tattoo, and peel off protective sheet.
2) Place tattoo picture-side down, against clear skin.
3) Wet back of tattoo thoroughly with sponge or cloth
4) Press firmly on back of tattoo for 30 seconds.
5) Peel off backing, rinse with water and let dry.

To remove, scrub with alcohol or cream cleanser.

KU-351-121

PaRragon

Bath New York Singapore Hong Kong Cologne Delhi Melbourne

First published by Parragon in 2007
Parragon
Queen Street House
4 Queen Street
Bath BA1 1HE, UK

Pirates of the Caribbean: At World's End
Based on characters created by Ted Elliott & Terry Rossio and Stuart Beattie and Jay Wolpert
Written by Ted Elliott & Terry Rossio
Based on Walt Disney's Pirates of the Caribbean
Produced by Jerry Bruckheimer
Directed by Gore Verbinski

ISBN 978-1-4054-9361-1
Printed in Italy

Can you get through the dragon tattoo maze
without hitting a dead end?

START

FINISH

Sao Feng has an important map and Barbossa wants it!
Use the special code to find out what is on the map.

A E F G H O R S T U

Will Turner wants the map, too.
He knows it leads to Davy Jones's Locker.

The pirates will attempt a voyage to Davy Jones's locker. To find out why, write every other letter on the lines below, starting with the letter T and going around the circle twice.

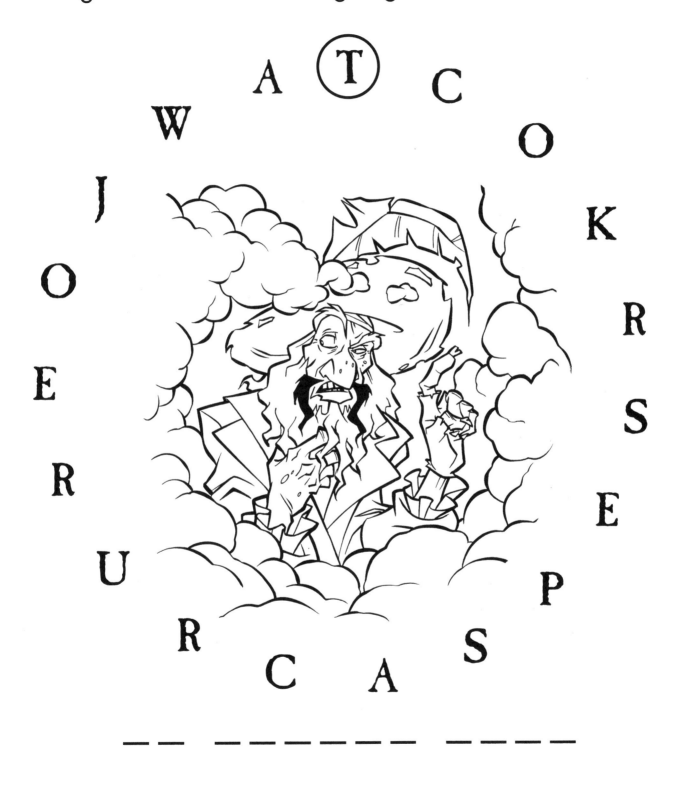

__ __ _____ ____

_____

Sword fight! The men from the East India Trading Company pull a surprise attack on the pirates!

Barbossa and the crew have a new ship.
Help them find the right path to it, so they can set sail and
rescue Jack.

1

2

3

To find out the name of their ship,
cross out every other letter starting with K.
Then write the letters that are left on the lines below.

K H V A J I D P F E M N C G

_ _ _   _ _ _ _

Meanwhile, somewhere in the Caribbean Sea, Davy Jones continues his endless journey aboard the *Flying Dutchman*.

Find two pairs that match exactly.

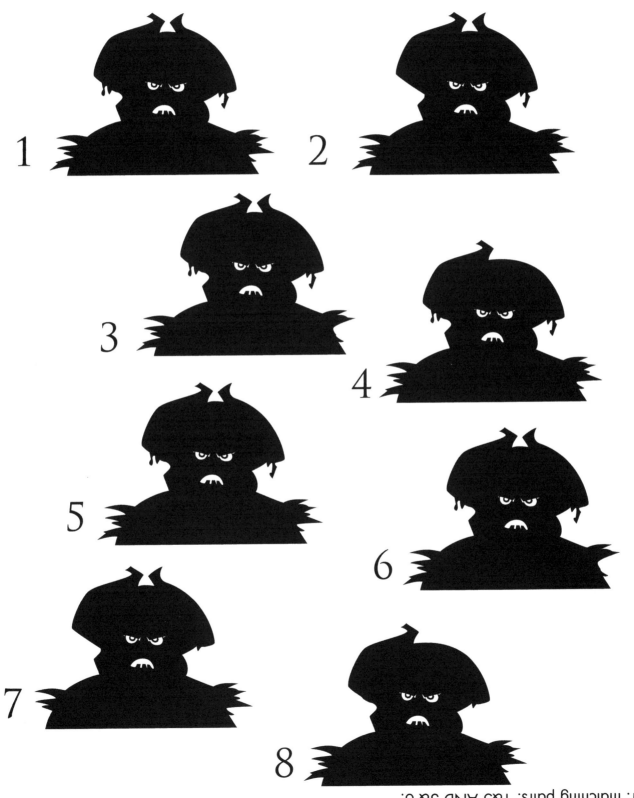

There's a riddle on the map to Davy Jones's Locker.
To uncover the secret message and learn the riddle, begin at
the letter O and write all the letters in order
in the spaces below.

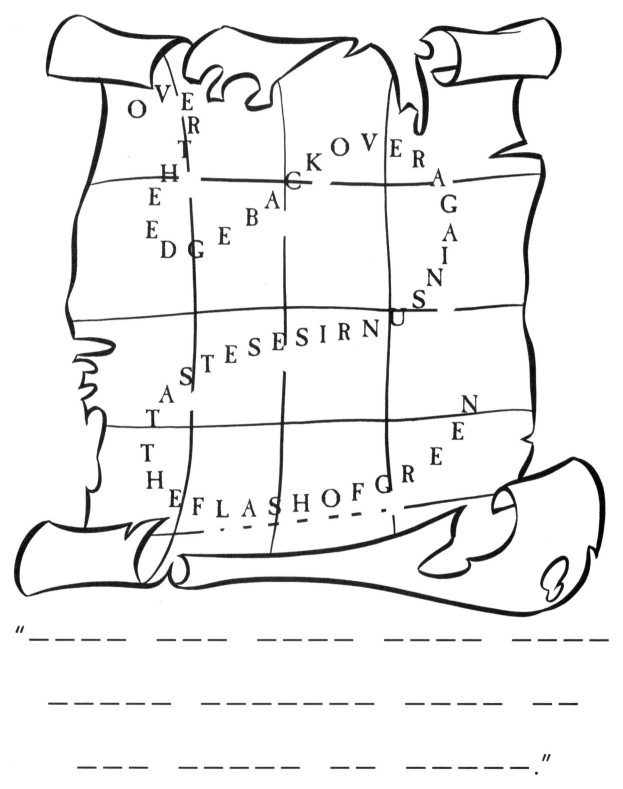

" _ _ _ _   _ _ _   _ _ _ _   _ _ _ _

_ _ _ _ _   _ _ _ _ _ _   _ _ _ _   _ _

_ _ _   _ _ _ _   _ _   _ _ _ _ _ ."

Meanwhile, Jack is still trapped in Davy Jones's Locker.
Can you make 20 words
using the letters in Davy Jones's Locker?

_____ _____ _____ _____ _____

_____ _____ _____ _____ _____

_____ _____ _____ _____ _____

_____ _____ _____ _____ _____

Look for more words!

At the edge of the world, the *Hai Peng* sails over the big waterfall.

The pirates survive the voyage, but the *Hai Peng* is shipwrecked. How many barrels can you count?

With a little help from the crabs, a new adventure is about to begin.

Using the grid as a guide, draw a picture of Jack Sparrow.

Look up, down, forwards, backwards and diagonally to find the names of everyone who wants to rescue Jack.

```
P D C N M G R B R
I I C O T J A D A
N G N T A R B M G
J I D T B Z L Y E
E B X O E A E T T
L B S C D L A R T
I S Z A B E H A I
A W I L L T K M X
H T E B A Z I L E
```

Jack Sparrow arrives, pirates-style! How many
times can you find the word CRAB in the puzzle?
Look up, down, forward, backward and diagonally.

B A R C R B C
B B A B A R C
A B A R C R R
R R C R A B A
C R A B C B B

The *Black Pearl* crew is back together again.
Look for 11 things that are different between the two pictures.

Answer:

With the crew back together, the *Black Pearl* sails again.

Ragetti's wooden eyeball is lost!
Can you find it hidden in the picture?

Jack finds a secret message on the map.
Hold this page up to a mirror to read it.

UP IS DOWN

"Up is down." Jack figures out the secret message!
The crew turns the *Black Pearl* upside down!

How many cannon balls can you count in the picture?

On the *Empress*, Elizabeth is treated like a queen.
Sao Feng's sword is somewhere in the room.
Can you find it?

After Soa Feng is hurt, he gives Elizabeth a gift.
To find out what it is called, cross out every letter that appears
five times. Then begin at the T and write the letters that are left
in order on the blanks as they appear from left to right.

T J H E R _ _ _

R C J A P _ _ _ _ _ _ _ _ ' _

T A R J I

J N S R K _ _ _ _

R N J O T

Sao Feng has made Elizabeth the new captain of the *Empress* and she quickly falls into the claws of Davy Jones.

The pirates declare war on the East India Trading Company!

Jack is taken prisoner on the *Flying Dutchman*.

Jack escapes and takes the Dead Man's Chest.

Barbossa asks Calypso for a favour, a really big favour!
To find out what Barbossa says, go around the circle twice
starting with the letter H,
then write every other letter in the lines below.

"_ _ _ _   _ _'

_ _ _ _   _ _   _ _ _ _

_ _ _   _ _ _ _!"

Help the pirates battle the East India Trading Company and show them the way through the maze.

START

FINISH